About Bill Copeland

For over 50 years Bill Copeland has been a "West Coast Airbrush Artist" coming out of the hot rod culture of the '50's and '60's Art found only in California. A contemporary of "Big Daddy Ed Roth" and "Von Dutch" Bill is especially well known for his T-shirt painting at car shows in America and Canada. His free style, concern for detail, and speed of painting anything a customer wanted on a t-shirt has forever exceeded anyone in his field. His custom artwork has been featured in magazines, calendars, maps, and hundreds of silkscreen T-shirt designs, as well as his contributions to publications, international companies, and movie studios. His murals have graced the sides of cars, vans, eighteen wheelers and buildings.

Today Bill Copeland's fine art canvas paintings are featured in his gallery and studio in Yucca Valley, California. He spends his time painting commissioned paintings and an occasional t-shirt (people don't wear his shirts anymore, they frame them).

"Bill Copeland has launched a thousand ships of the highway, each lovingly detailed with murals or pinstriping…"
RoadKing Magazine

"Bill Copeland fired up the airbrush, and turned on his creative series."
Street Rodder Magazine

"Bill Copeland is one of the leading artists in the country…He has a way of turning people on with his own special brand of wildness."
Vans & Trucks Magazine

"Bill Copeland's identifiable style of art has developed a legion of followers on the West Coast."
T-Shirt Retailer Magazine

Bill Copeland Gallery and Art Studio
55940 Twentynine Palms Hwy. #3, Yucca Valley, CA 92284
revbillcopeland@yahoo.com • www.billcopelandgallery.com

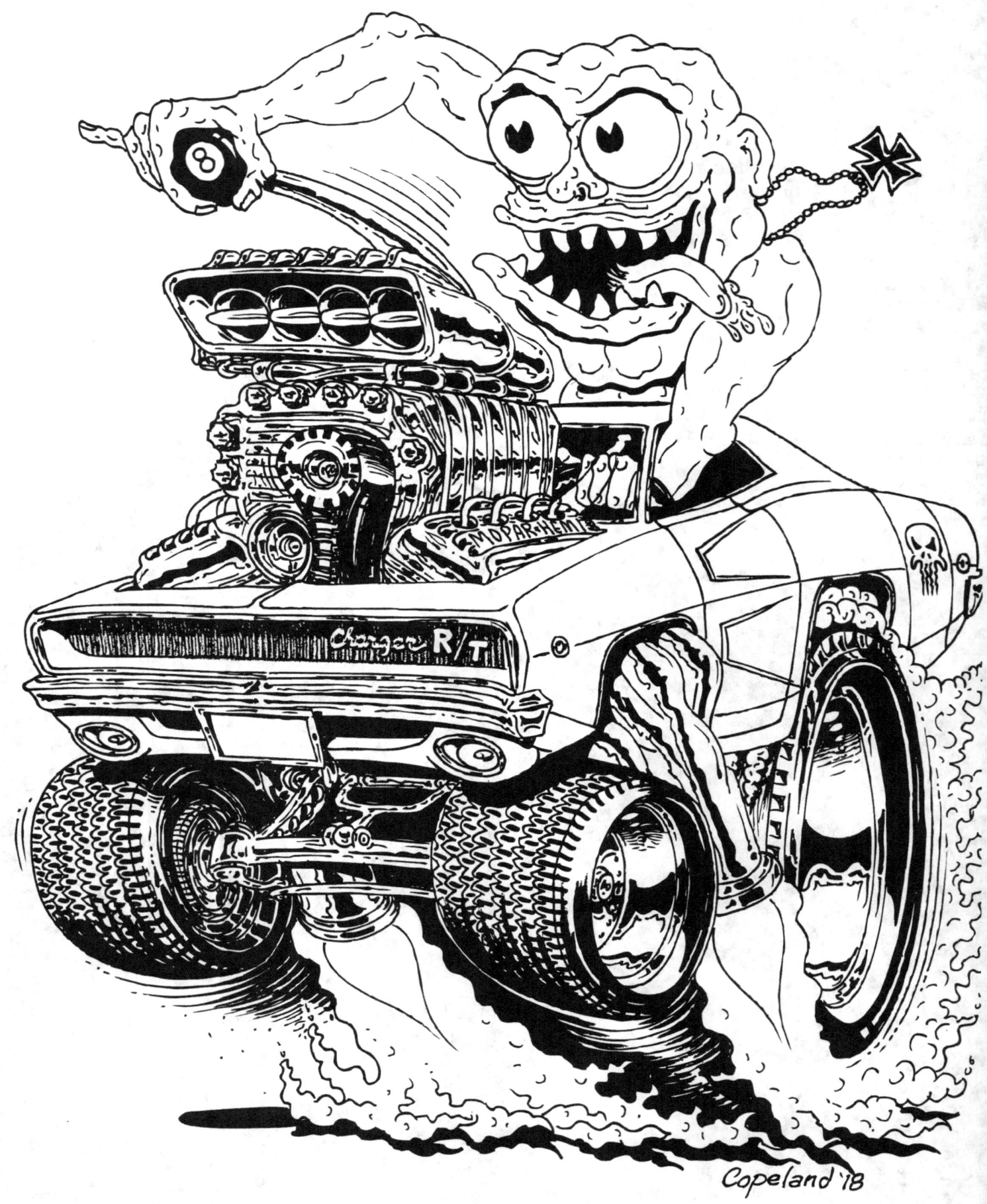

Copeland '18

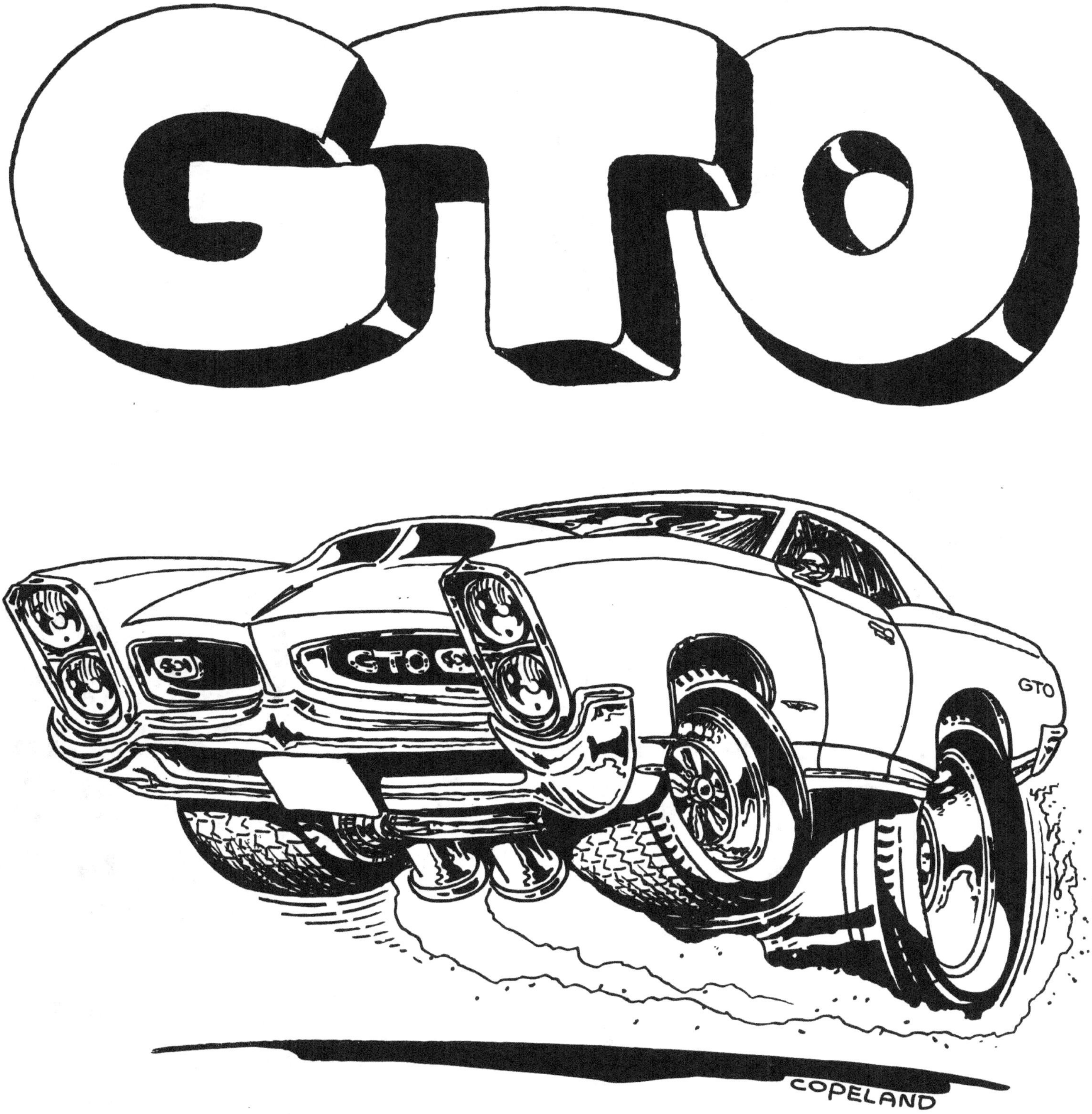

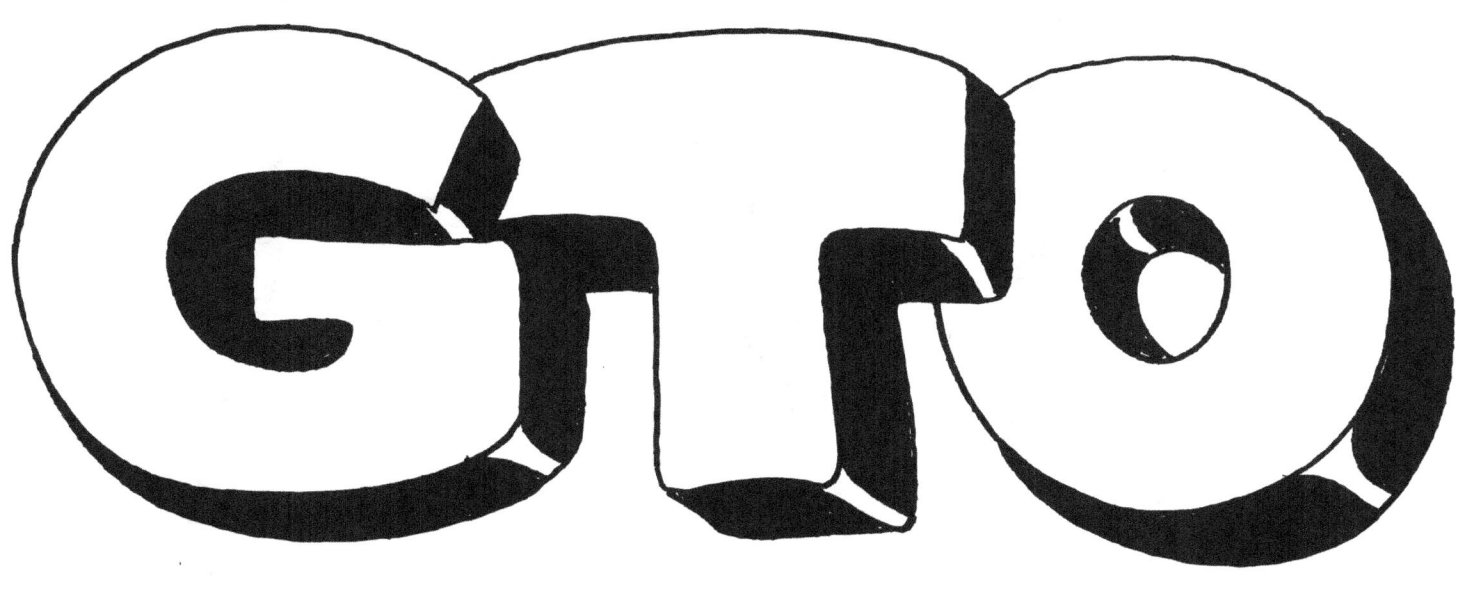

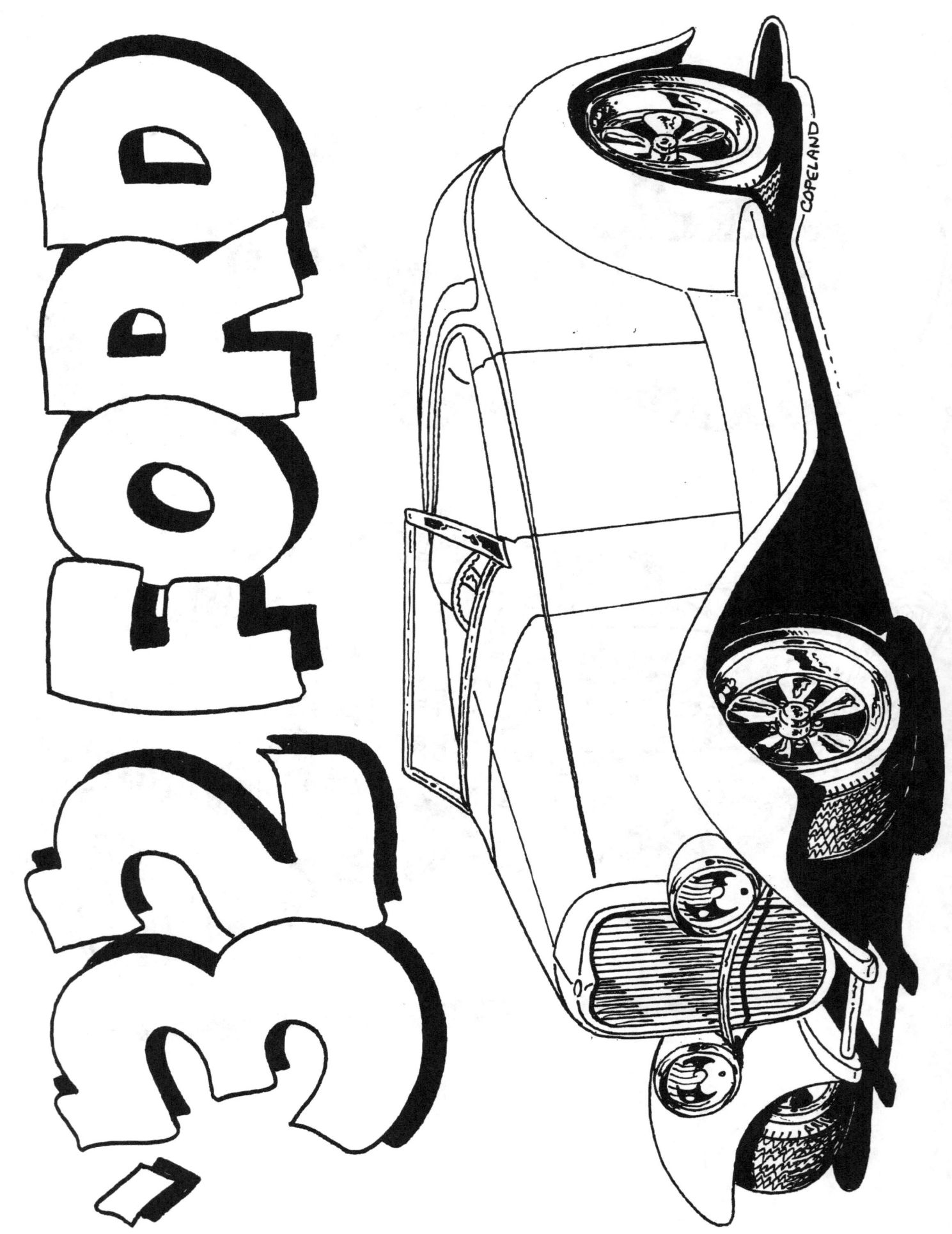

STREET ROD
FORD

COPELAND

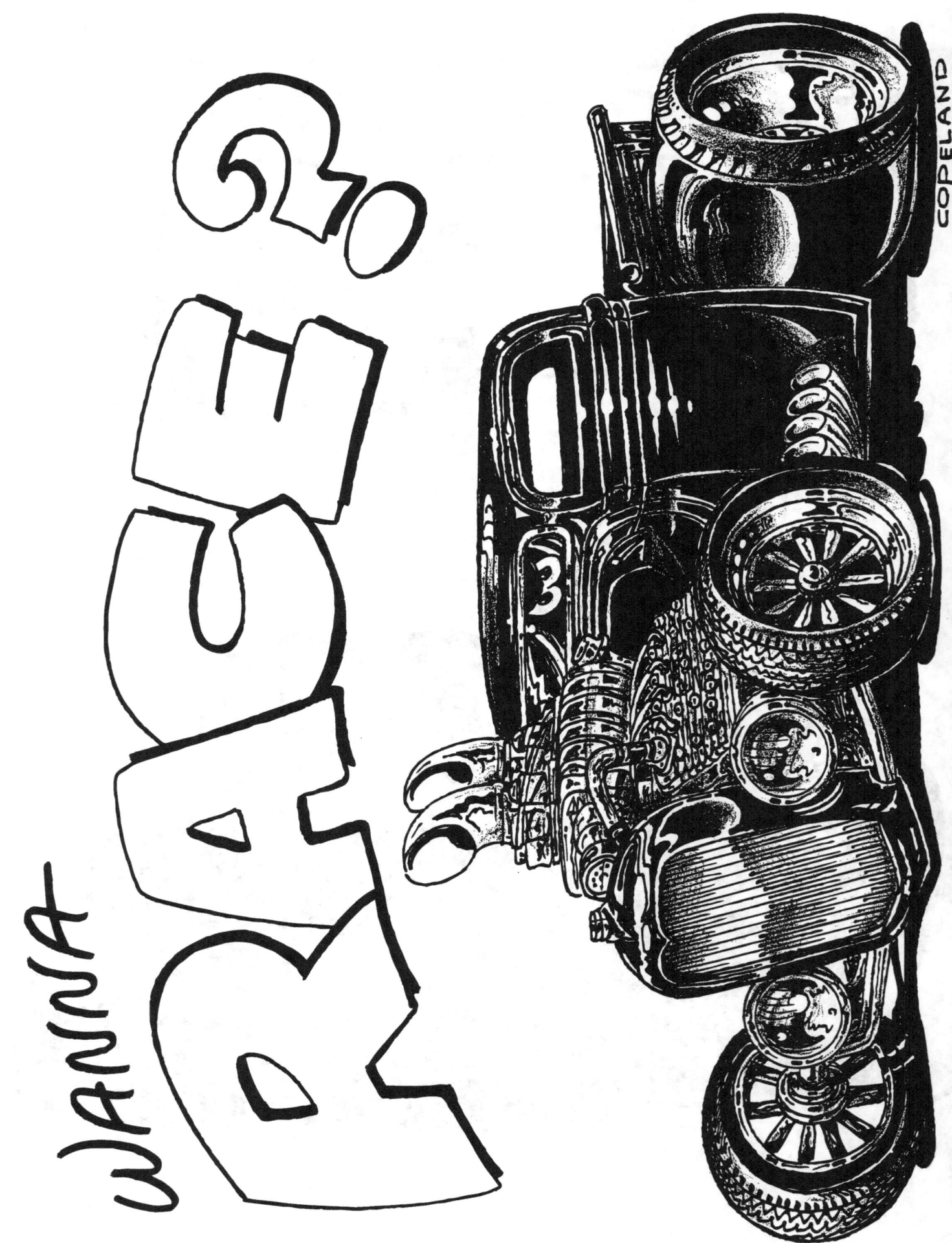

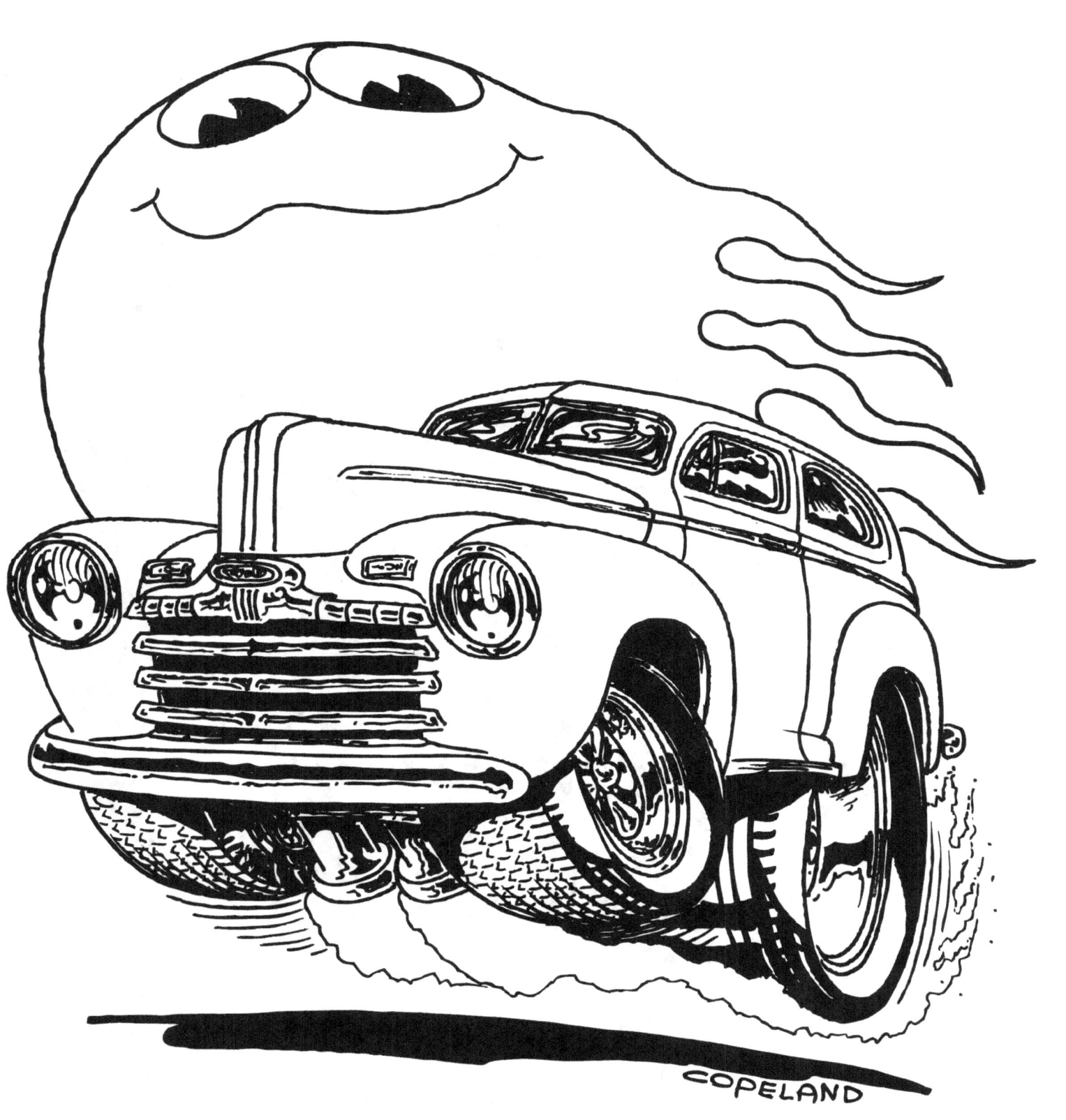

COPELAND

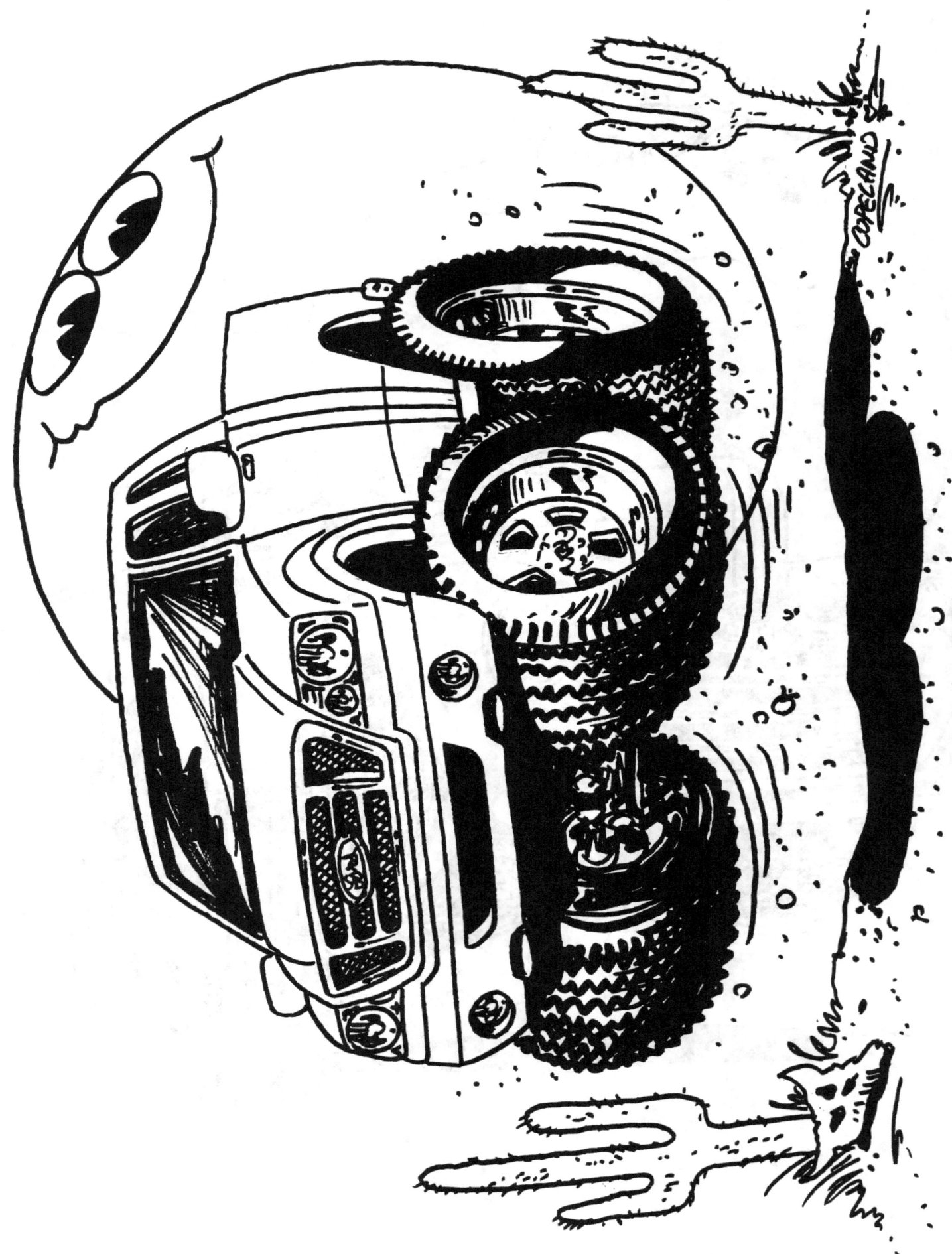

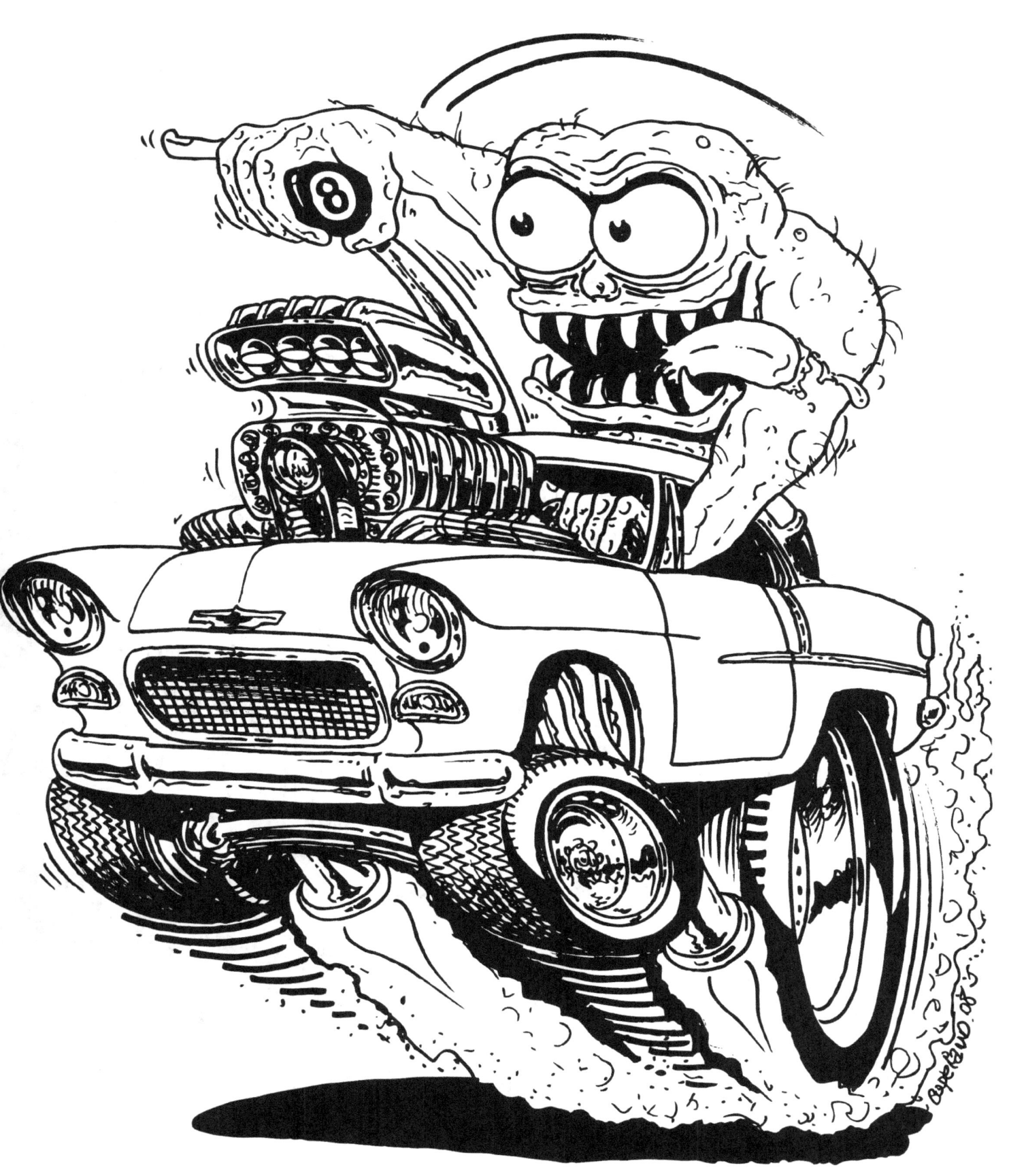

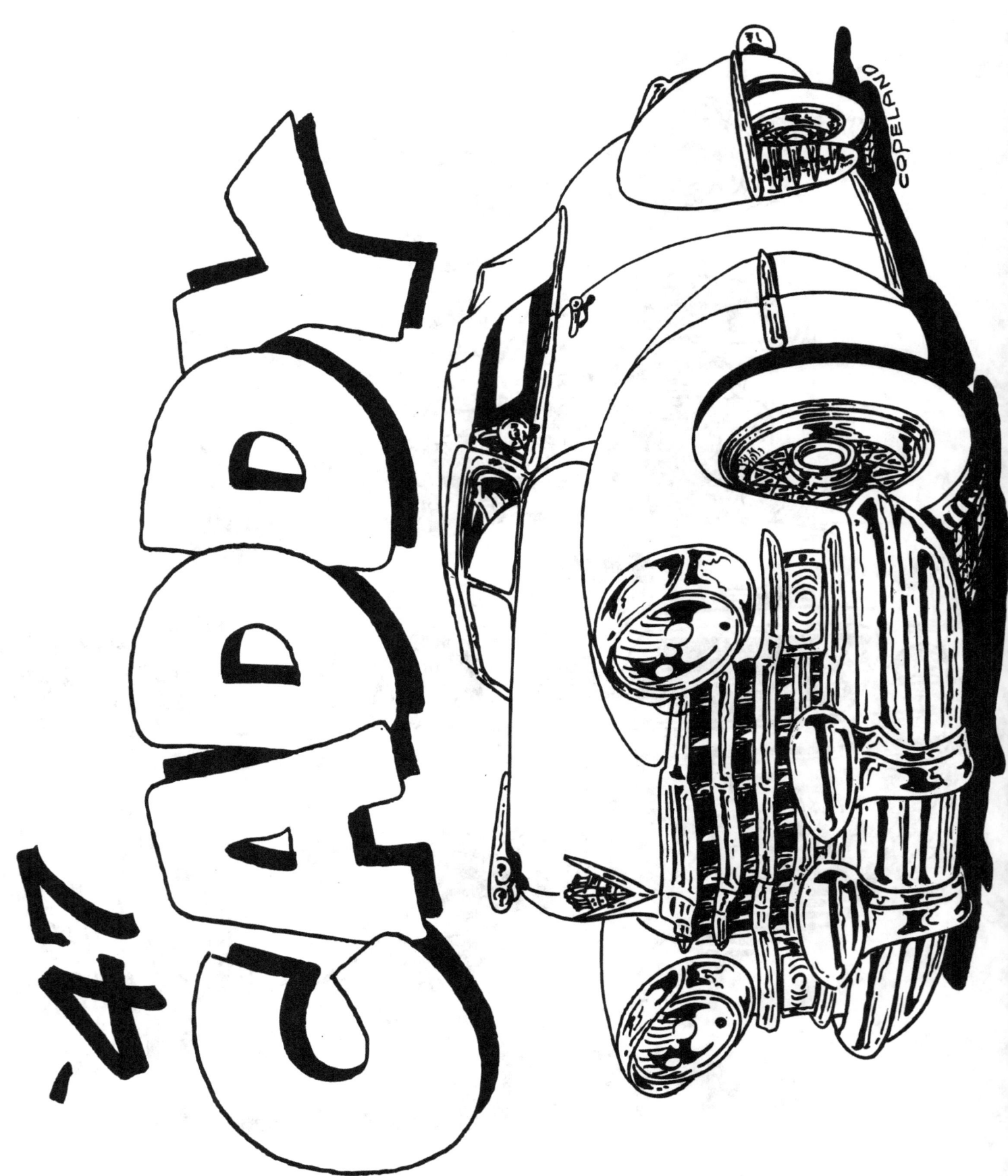

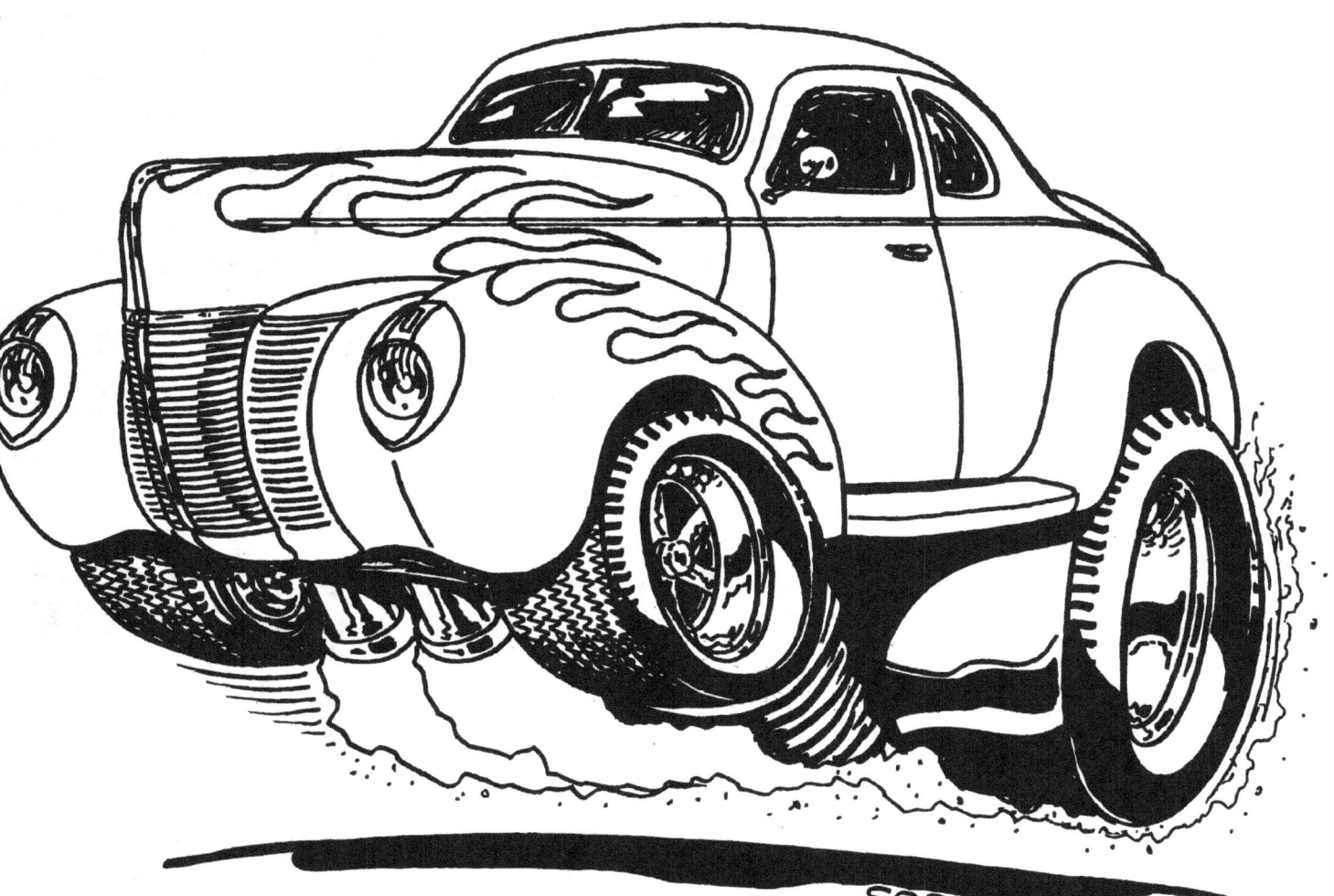

'61 CHEVY NOMAD

'40 FORD

COPELAND

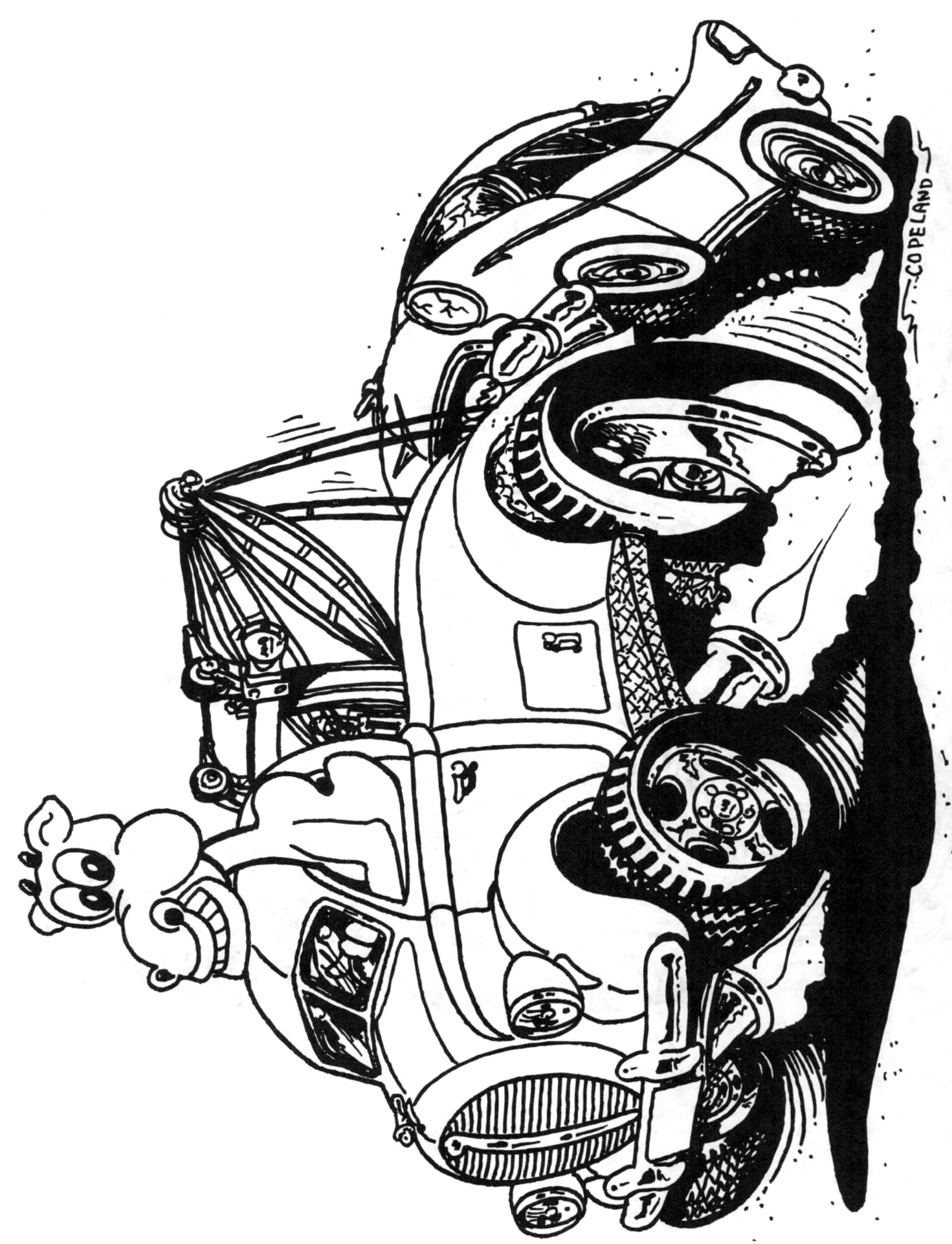

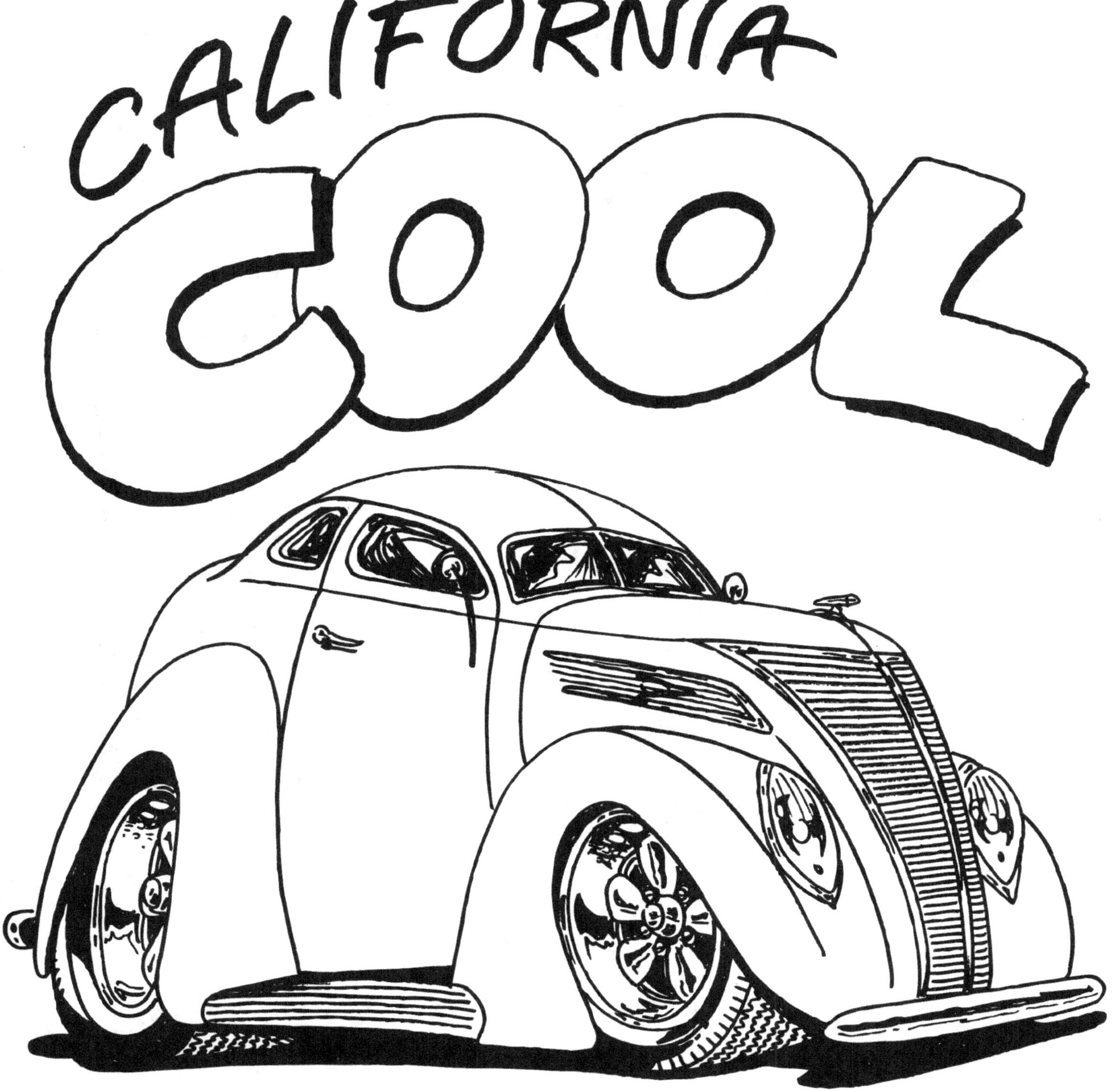
CALIFORNIA
COOL

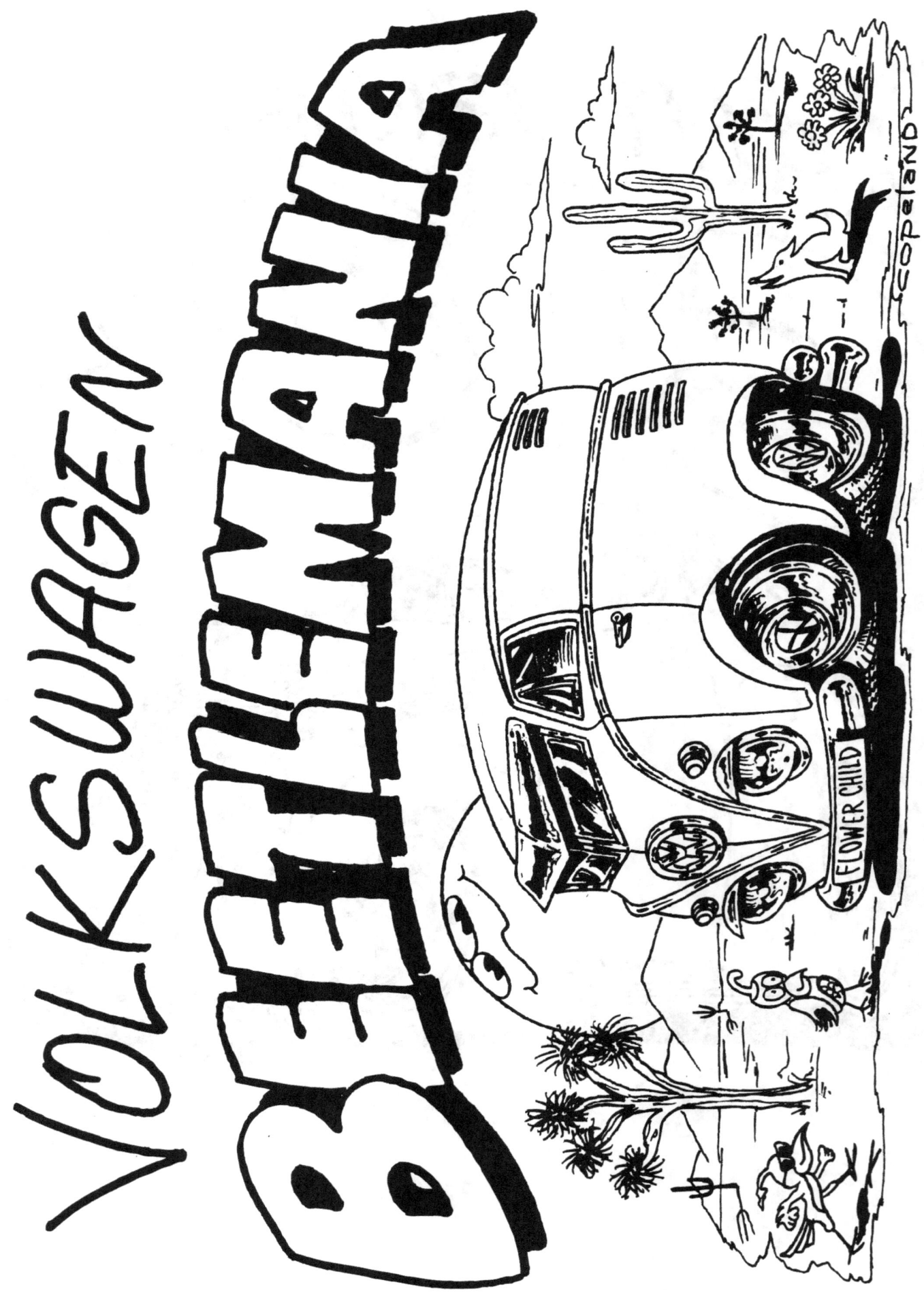

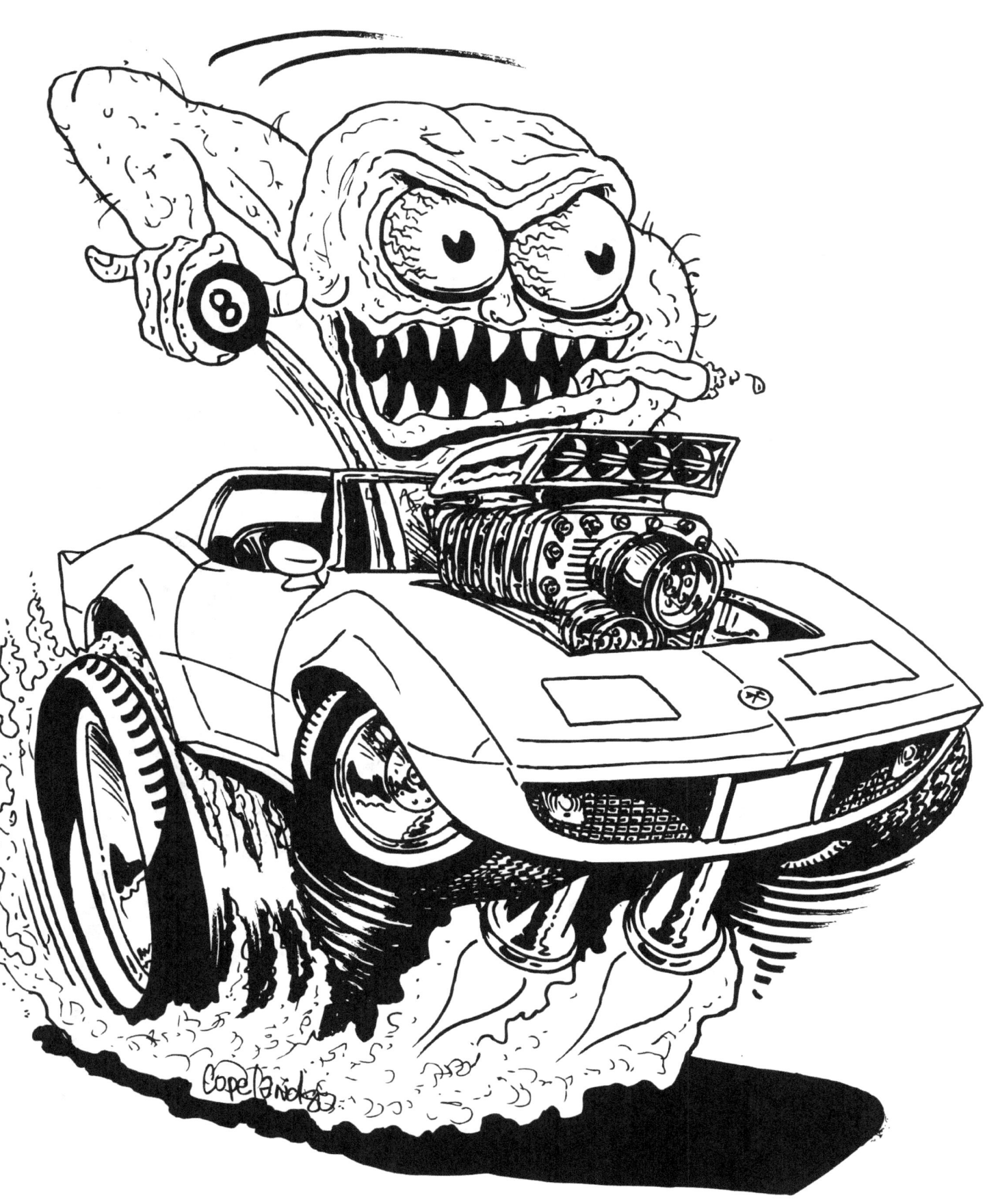

HOT ROD TANK

Copeland

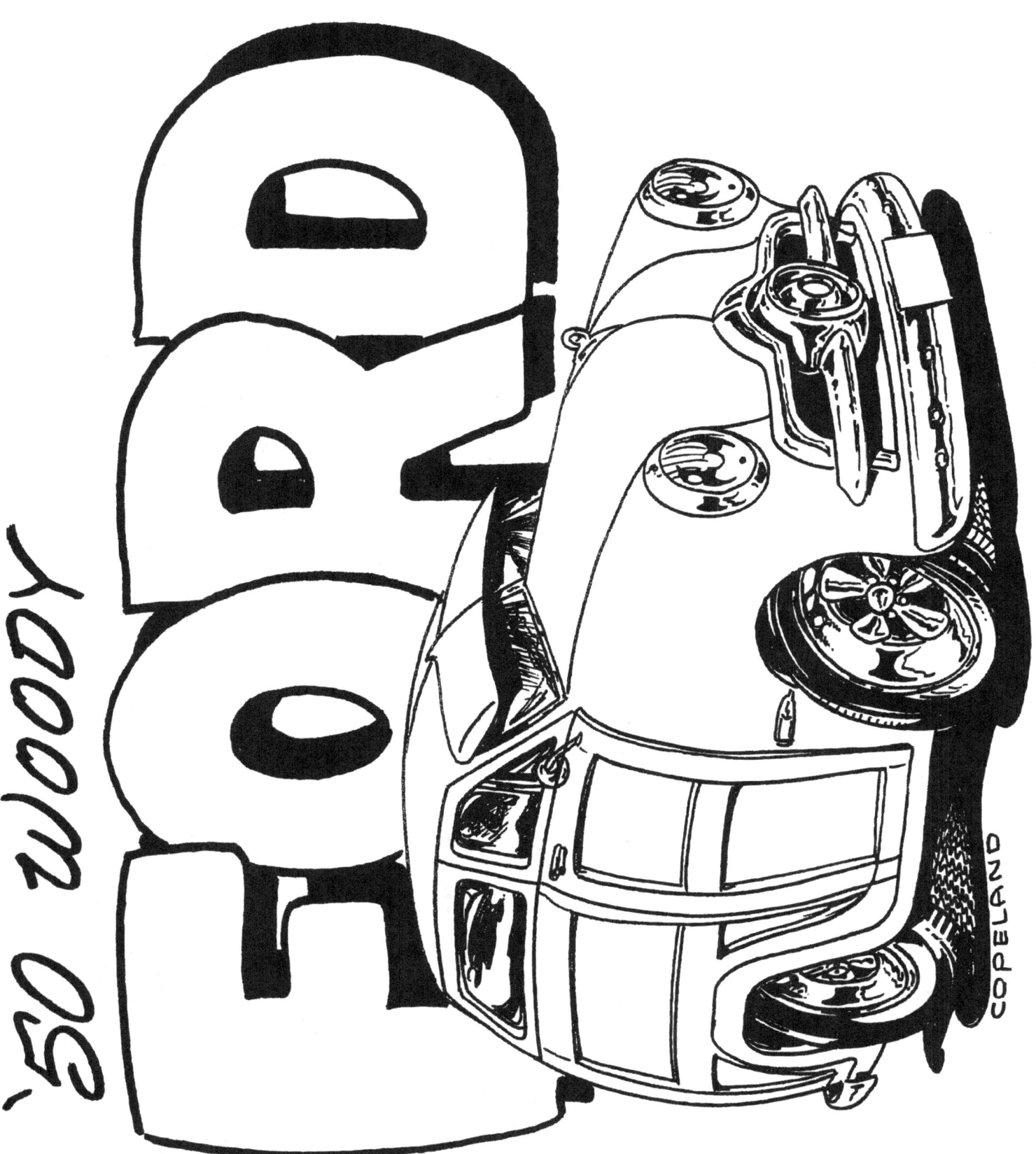

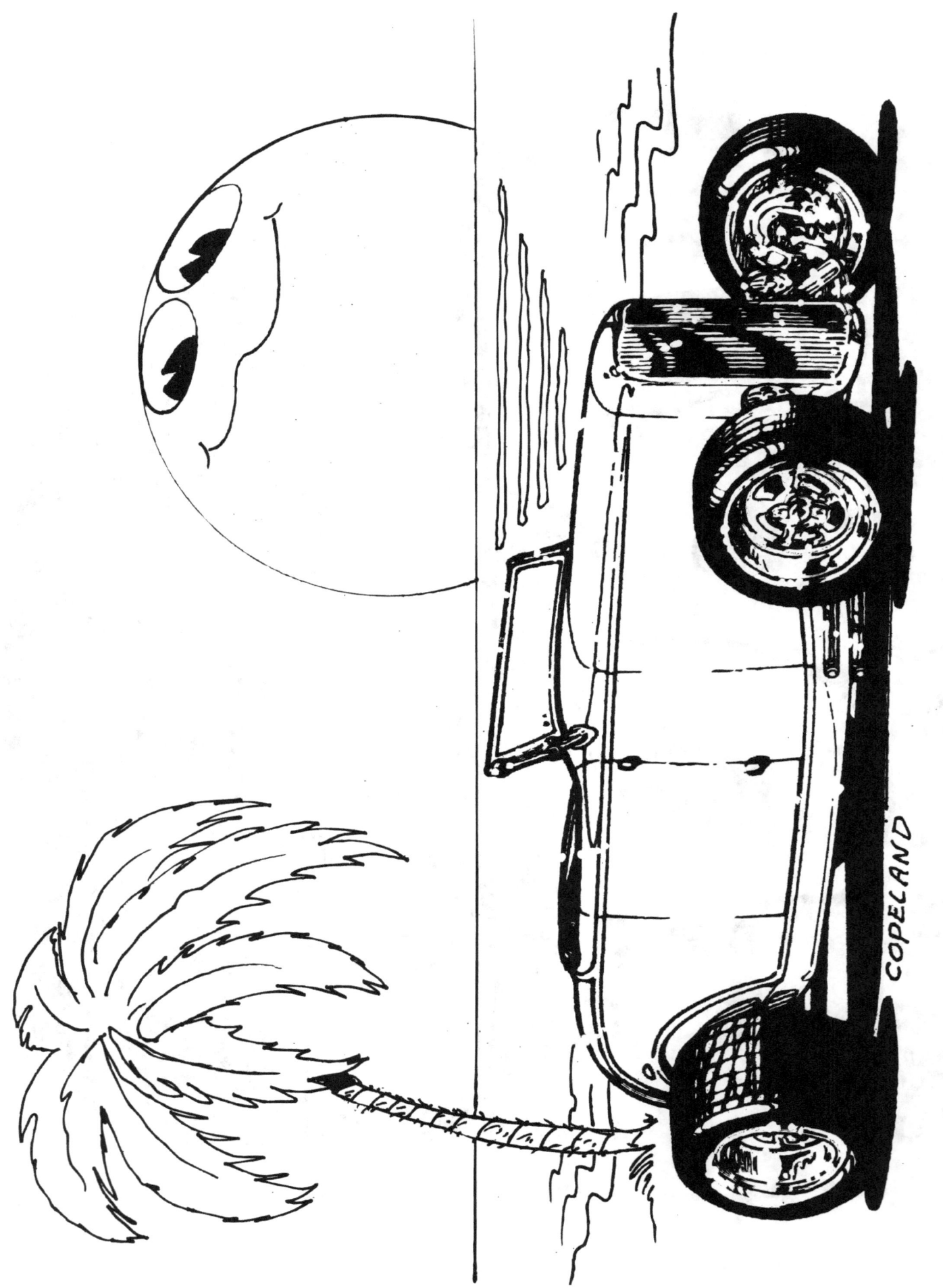

WILD '55 CHEVY

STYLIN' EL CAMINO

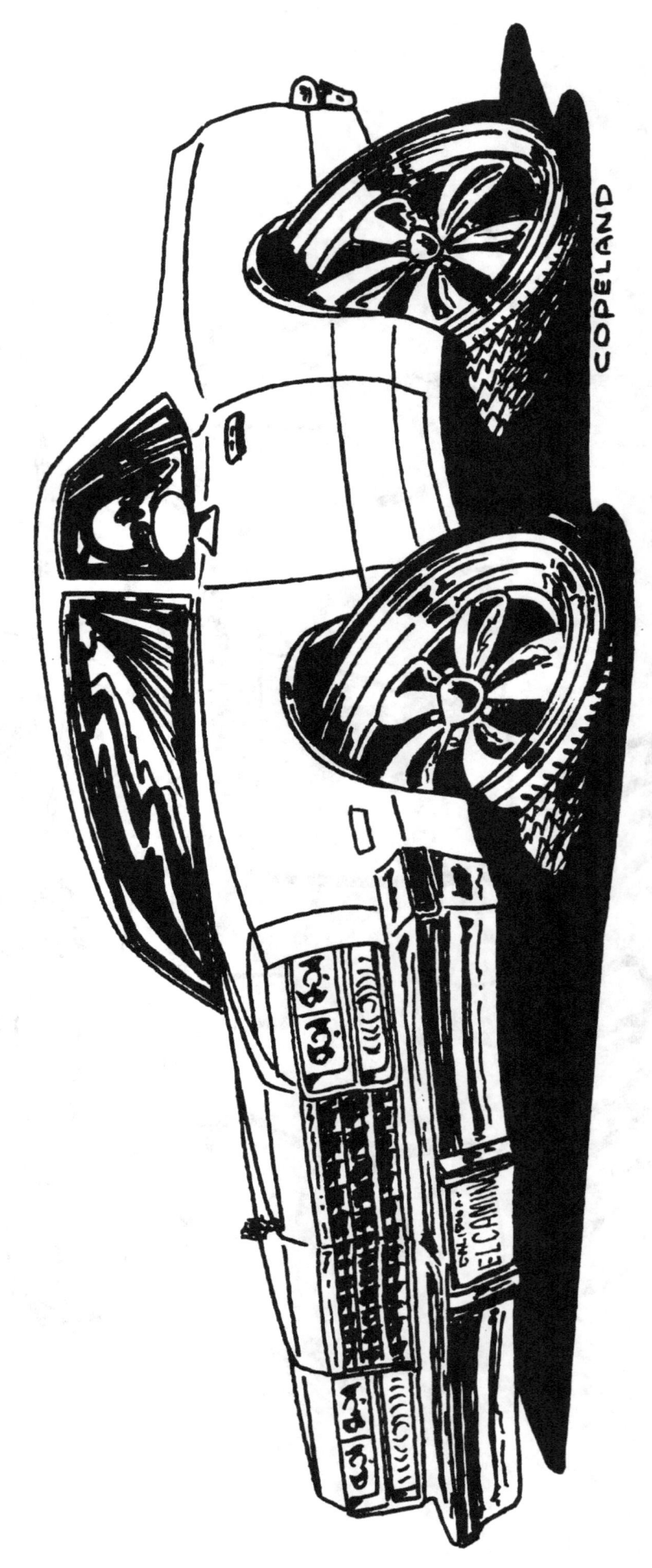

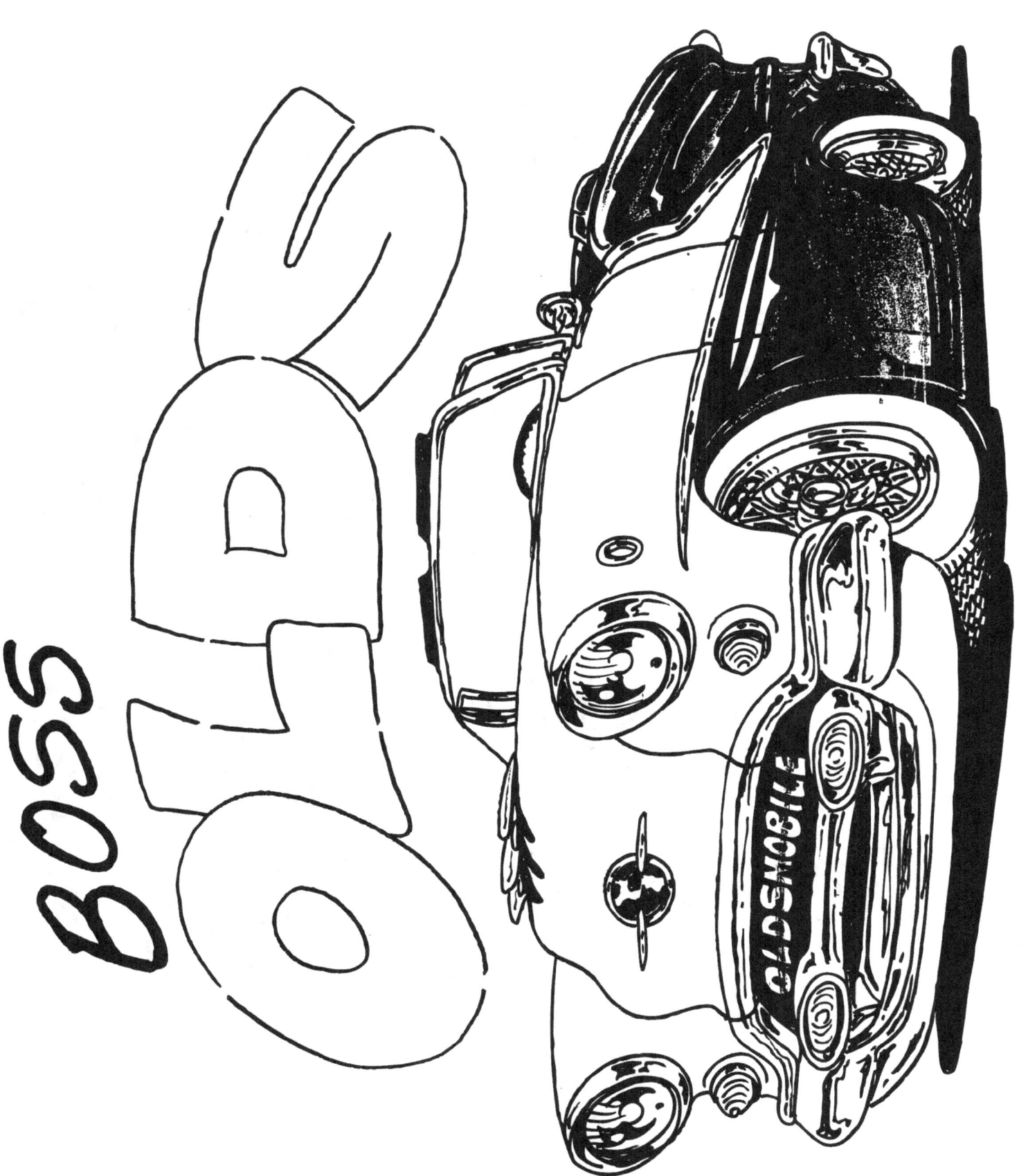

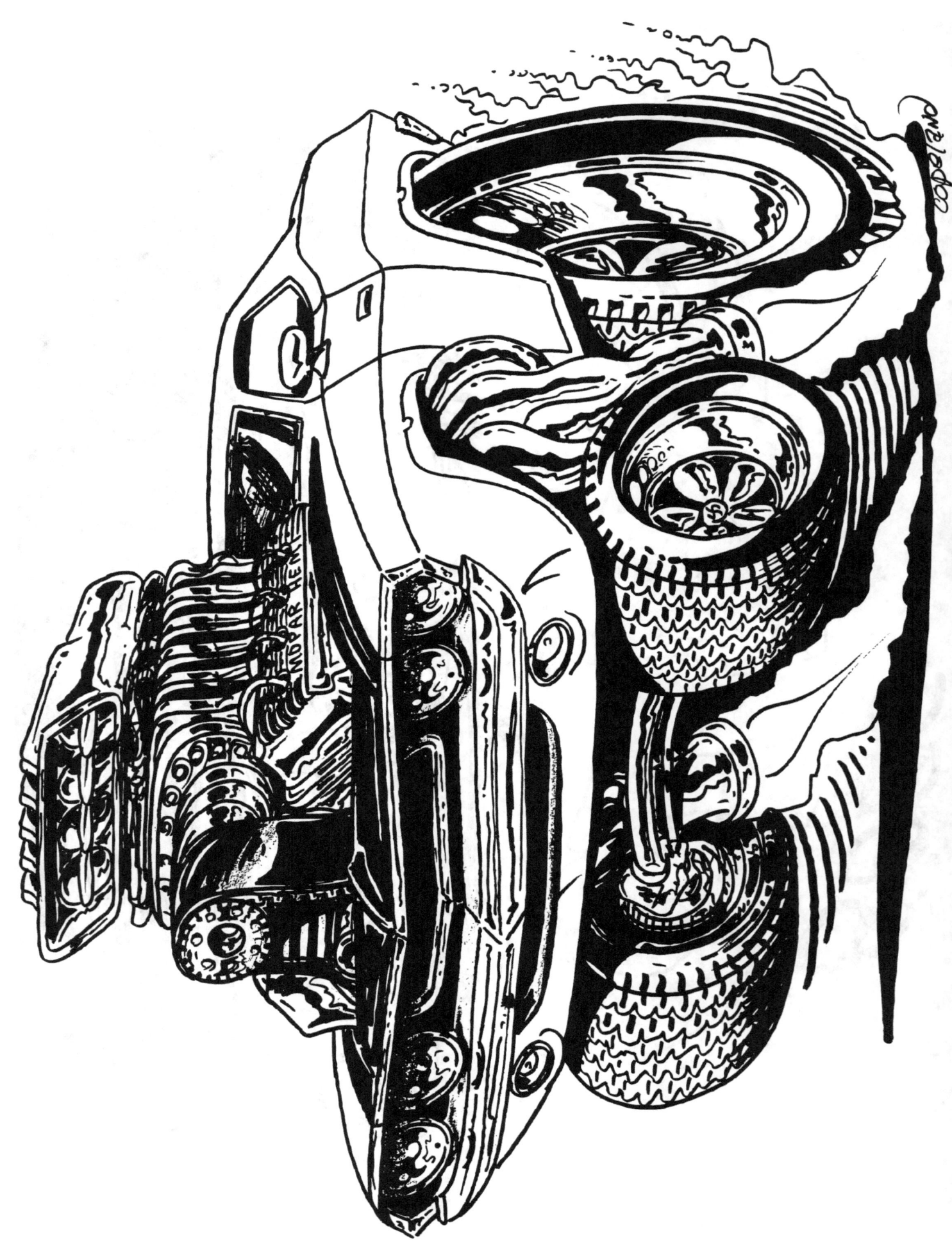

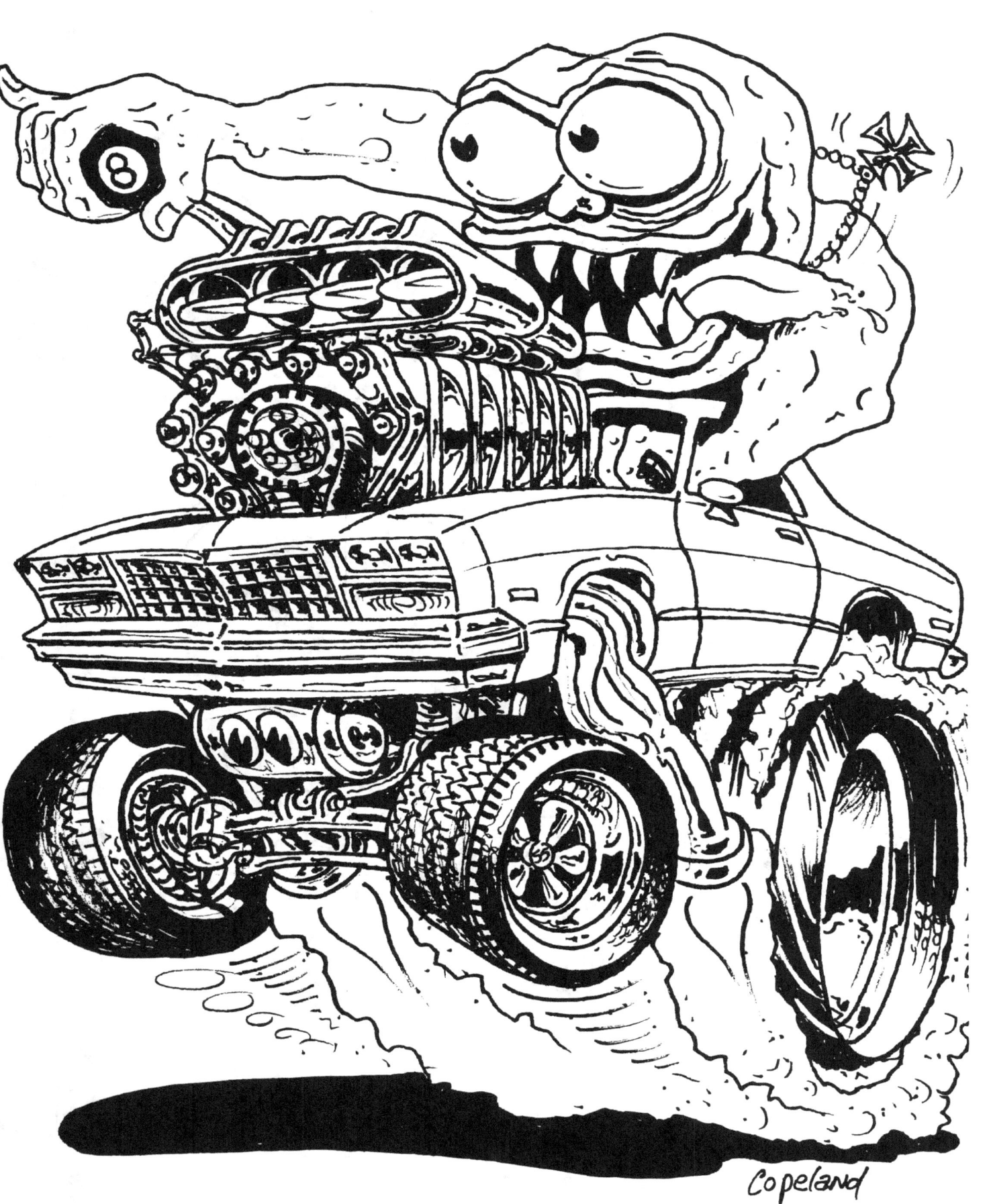

Copeland

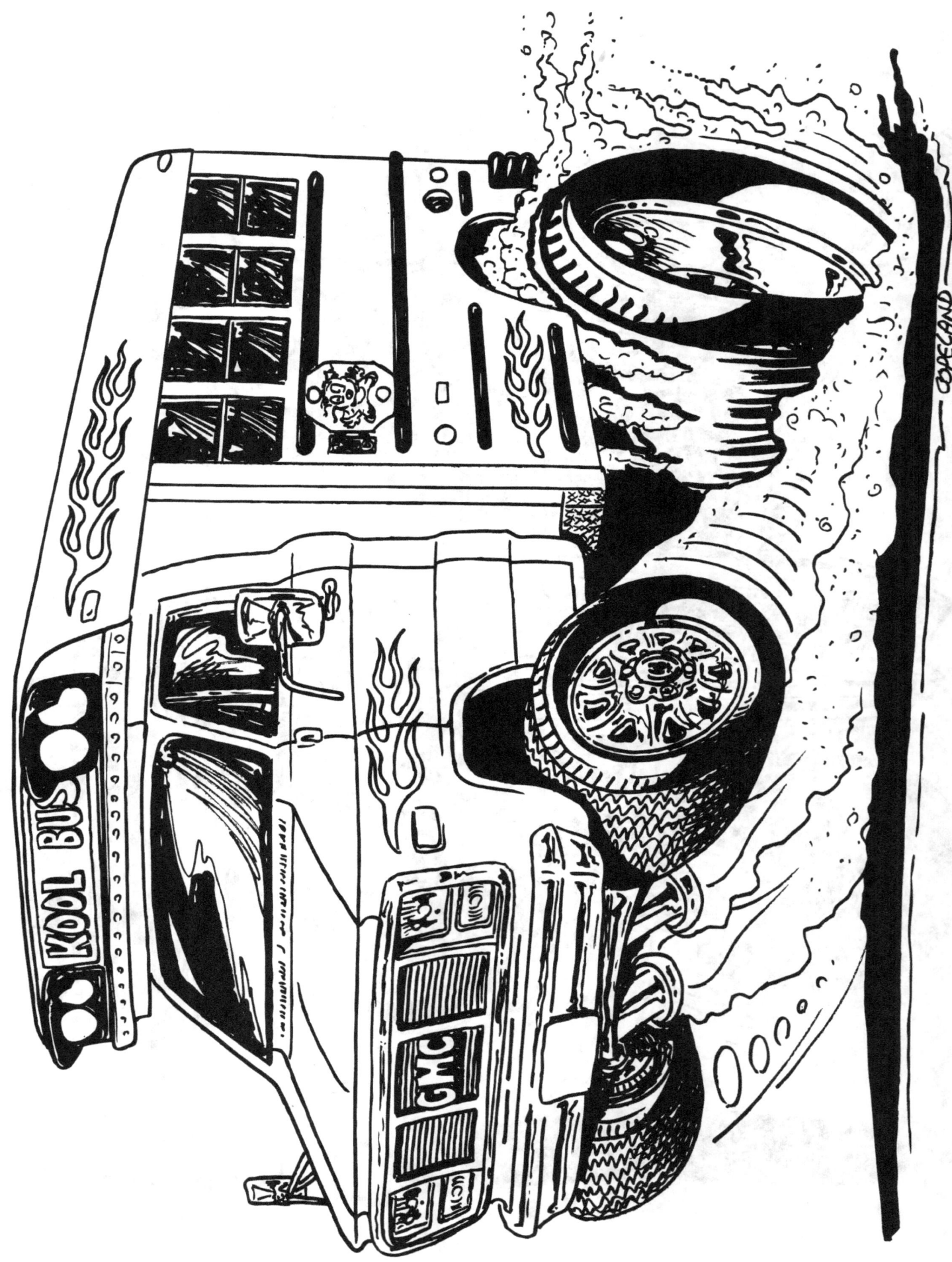

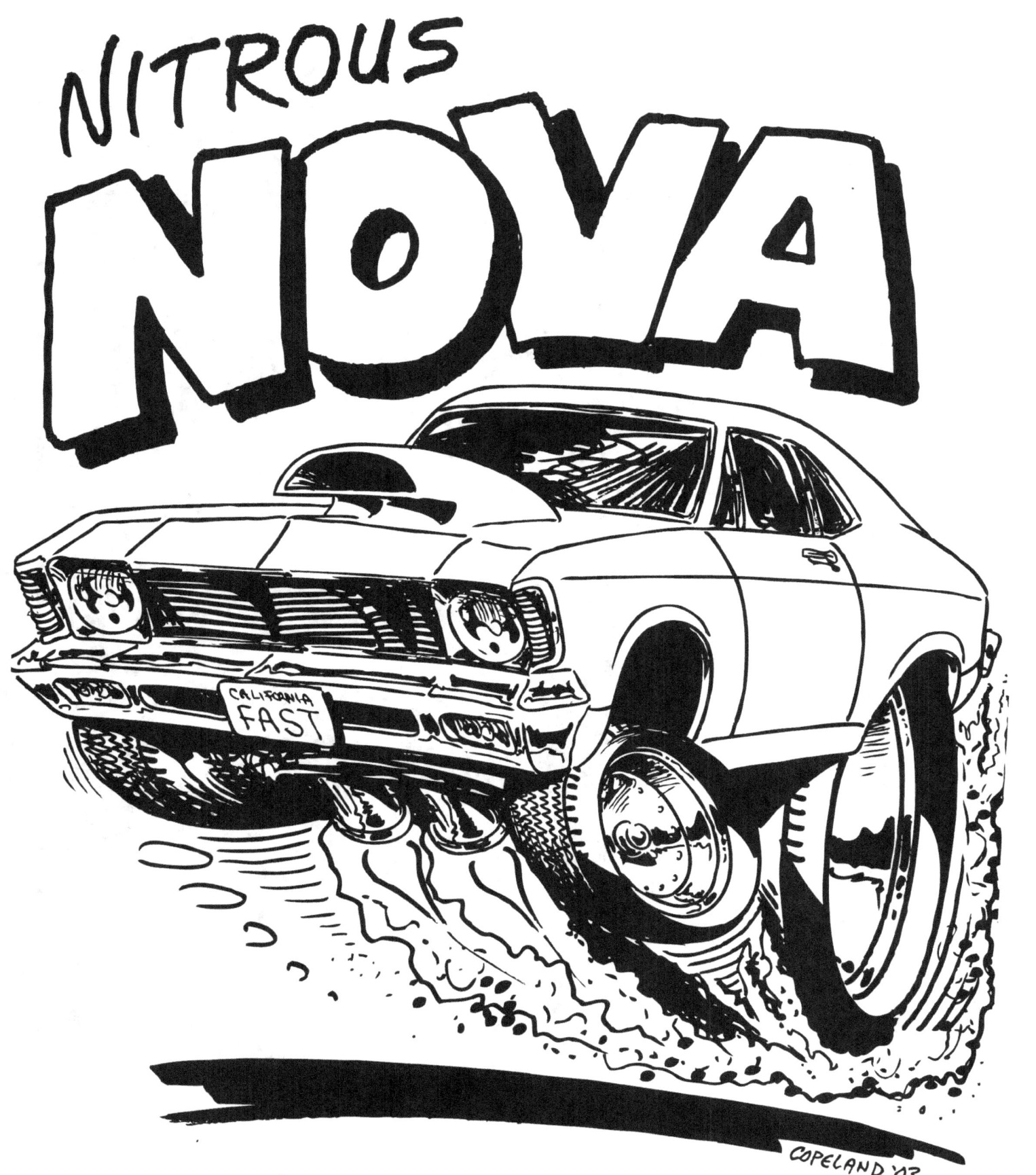

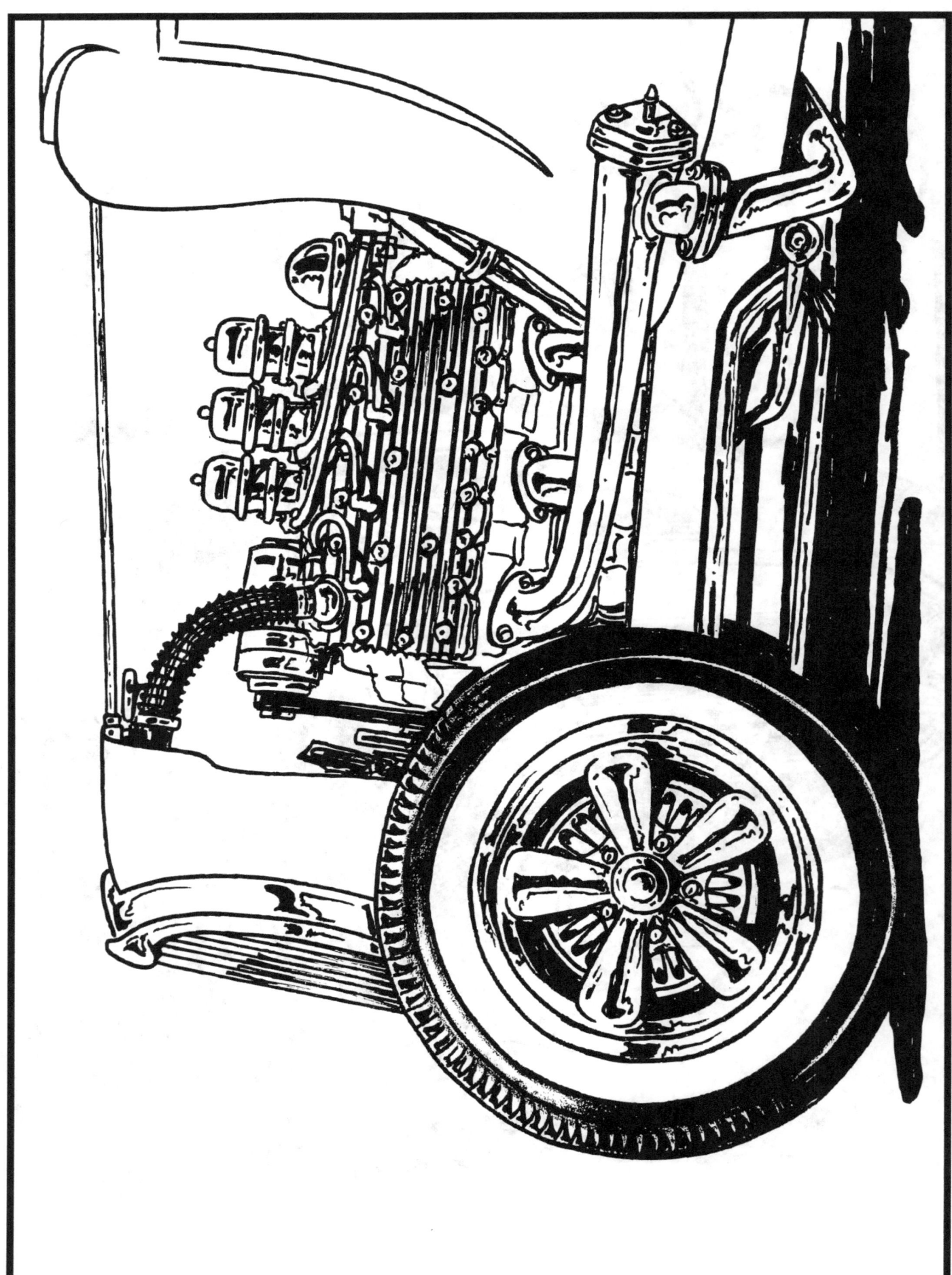